AWESOMELY FUNNY HUMOR...

Why do they have recess in tough schools?
To evacuate the wounded.

What do you do when you see an elephant going?
Swim for your life.

Why did the cannibals capture the Olympic team?
They love fast food.

IN *AWESOMELY GROSS JOKES!*

Awesomely GROSS JOKES

By Julius Alvin

ZEBRA BOOKS
KENSINGTON PUBLISHING CORP.

ZEBRA BOOKS

are published by

Kensington Publishing Corp.
475 Park Avenue South
New York, NY 10016

First Zebra Books printing: August, 1988

Printed in the United States of America

To Jerry and Gloria, who've proved that love can triumph over any adversity. Thanks for making life more special for your family that loves you.

ACKNOWLEDGEMENT

To the creative and very comic mind of Alan Wexler, for his important contribution to this book.

CONTENTS

Chapter One

GROSS ETHNIC AND RACIAL JOKES

Why is a car engine like an Italian girl?

On a cold morning when you really need it, it won't kick over.

What's another name for an Arab who tends sheep?

A pimp.

What do you get when you cross a JAP and a computer?

A system that never goes down.

Why did the redneck go out every night and jerk off the dog?

To feed his cat.

One Russian walked up to his friend on the street and asked, "Did you hear that Ivan Patronov died?"

"Died?" his friend said with surprise. "I didn't even know he'd been arrested."

What's the most popular new name for a Ukrainian baby?

"Thing."

The Dean of the university was walking by the Psychology Building one day when he saw a team of workmen unloading six foot high cages and carrying them inside. Wondering what they were doing, he entered and walked to the office of the chairman of the Psychology Department.

"Professor," he asked. "What are you doing with those huge cages?"

"They're for our research program next semester. We're using Polacks for our electric shock experiments."

"Polacks? I thought you used rats."

"We did," the department chairman replied, "but we just get too damned attached to the rats."

Why did the Polack return the necktie?

It was too tight.

What kind of drugs do JAPs snort?

Diet Coke.

Why do Jewish husbands die young?

They want to.

Did you hear about the Polish lottery?

The winner gets a dollar a year for a million years.

What do you call a Polack with a five hundred dollar hat?

Pope.

A company president decides he needs a new building, so he calls some contractors in to submit bids. The first guy he talks to is Polish.

"You've had a chance to look at the plans," he says. "How much will it cost to build?"

"Two million," replies the Polish contractor. "One million for materials, one million for labor."

The company president thanks the Polack, and calls in an Italian contractor.

The Italian's bid is four million.

"How would you break that down?" the company president asks.

"Two million for materials, two million for labor," the Italian replies.

The company president dismisses him, then calls in the third man, a Jewish contractor.

"How much are you bidding?" the president asks.

"Six million."

"Six million? That's very high. How do you break that down?"

"It's simple," said the Jewish contractor. "Two million for me, two million for you, and two million for the Polack."

Did you hear about the New Wave Japanese garden?

It's full of punk rocks.

What do Hawaiian women use as I.U.D.s?

Hula hoops.

Why did the Polack run out of the bullfights?

When the matador screamed "Toro!", he went home to get his lawn mower.

Why did the Polack woman think she was having an illegal abortion?

The doctor was wearing a mask.

What do WASPs call a handjob?

A manicure.

What's a Polish handjob?

A girl sucks your fingers.

What do rednecks usually call the first girl they screw?

"Sis."

Why do Polacks all wear turtlenecks?

To cover up their flea collars.

What's the difference between a Russian woman and a bowling ball?

If worse came to worse, you could eat the bowling ball.

What's the difference between blacks and radial tires?

Radial tires don't sing spirituals when you put chains on them.

Did you hear about the Mississippi town that couldn't decide between starting a chapter of the Klu Klux Klan and organizing a baseball league?

They compromised by hunting down blacks and beating them to death with bats.

What's the first thing a WASP wife does after sex?

Moves.

What kind of sexual lubricant do racists use?

KKK-Y jelly.

Why did the Polack go to the Chinese Hand Laundry?

He'd just beat off, and he wanted to get cleaned up.

Why did so many Mexicans surround the Alamo?

The Texans kept beating them off.

What did the Polack do when he wanted music to dance in his head?

Bought a headband.

Two Polacks were out in a boat fishing. They discovered a great spot where the fish were really biting. When it was time to go, one Polack suggested that they mark the spot so they could find it the next day.

"How we gonna do that?" the other Polack asked.

"Simple. I'll just put an X on the bottom of the boat," replied the first guy. He started to take off his clothes to jump in when his friend said, "Wait, Stanislow. What if we don't get the same boat tomorrow?"

A man was walking down the road when he spotted a Polish farmer holding a pig up by its hind legs so that it could eat apples off a tree. He watched in amazement for a moment, then decided to approach the Polack.

"Excuse me," he said. "I think you'd save a lot of time if you gave the tree a shake, then let the pig eat the apples that fall to the ground."

The Polack shrugged. "What's time to a pig?"

What do you call 17 Polacks standing in a circle?

A dope ring.

Why did the Italian hang a big "Cash Only" sign around his neck when he was on safari?

He wanted to keep wild animals from charging.

The Polish government decided to enhance its prestige by building the longest bridge in the world for an underdeveloped country. So Polish engineers constructed a span all the way over the Sahara Desert.

Instead of prestige, however, all the Polish government got was ridicule. They decided to send a team of engineers to Africa to tear down the structure. But when the bridge demolition team arrived, they reported they couldn't touch the structure.

"Your orders are to go ahead and blow it up," shouted the president of Poland.

"Okay," said the head engineer. "But we're gonna kill a couple thousand Italians who are fishing off it."

Did you hear about the German girl who was being raped by ten Polacks?

She screamed, "Nein! Nein!" So one of the Polacks left.

Why do blacks have such strong arms?

Color TVs are getting heavier.

Why are newborn Russian babies so appealing these days?

They have that certain glow.

A Polack went to the bordello and said to the madam, "I want to sleep with Irma."

The madam went over to the blonde, talked for a moment, then said, "Irma wants $200."

"But it was only $50 last time?"

The madam shrugged. "Take her or leave her."

The Polack paid the money and took Irma upstairs. Afterwards, when he was putting his pants on, he asked the whore, "Well, how was I?"

Irma replied, "You're absolutely the worst lay I ever had in my life, just like I told you the last time. I can't understand why you came back?"

"I wanted a second opinion," replied the Polack.

What's the most popular sitcom in Kiev?

My Three Heads.

What's the most popular soap opera in Kiev?

The Young and the Radioactive.

Why do Chinamen walk around with their flies open one day a year?

Because it's "Erection" Day.

Why did the Italian want to become a gynecologist?

He was very interested in the openings in that field.

Why did they install TV sets in Polish ballparks?

So the fans could see what's going on in their local bar.

What sound does the new Cadillac make when you hit the horn?

"Honkey."

Why do Polacks love girls with big noses?

Easy pickings.

Did you hear about the Polack who opened a topless bar?

A week of rain bankrupted him.

How did the Germans capture Poland so easily?

They marched in backwards and said they were leaving.

What goes "hop, skip, jump, boom?"

Nicaraguan children playing in a mine field.

What's the definition of a virgin El Salvadorean soldier?

One who hasn't raped a nun.

How do soldiers in El Salvador keep their bayonets sharp?

They keep a dead baby on the tip.

How do they take the census in El Salvador?

They add up the number of arms and legs and divide by 2.

What's the South African police's version of the Miranda warning?

"You have the right to remain dead. . . ."

Did you hear about the Polish baby who was hurt at his baptism?

Some one flushed.

How can you tell a Polish tourist in New York?

He's the guy trying to buy a condom from a bag lady.

Where do black kids get all that money for crack?

From your kids.

Did you hear about the Japanese factory that painted all its robots black?

The next day, they were all in the john smoking dope.

The teacher was giving a lesson on gardening. She picked up an implement and asked, "What is this, class?"

"Dat a shovel," came the reply.

"Good. And what's this?" she asked, holding up a rake.

Again, someone answered correctly. But when she held up the third tool, all she got was silence. Finally, she announced, "Class, this is a hoe."

Little Amos looked at her in disgust. "Hell, that ain't no hoe. My sister's a hoe, and she don't look nothing like that."

What do you get when you cross a black and a WASP?

An abortion.

What do you call a 200 pound Italian woman?

Anorexic.

Two black politicians met on Capitol Hill. One said to the other, "Did you hear that Reagan's finally convinced the South Africans to accept a black American ambassador?"

"That's good news," the second politican said. "But did you hear the bad news?"

"No."

"The black dude's got to have AIDS."

The Jewish woman and the black man had a little boy. One day, the boy came home from school obviously distressed. "What's wrong?" his mother asked.

"I've gotta know if I'm more Jewish or more black," the boy said.

"That's a tough one, son," the mother said. "Why don't you ask your father."

The little boy waited until Dad came home from work. When he popped the question, his father demanded to be told why he wanted to know.

"You see, Freddy down the street has a bike to sell. I don't know whether to bargain him down or just wait until dark and steal it."

Why is teenage sex so exciting in Beirut?

When you screw in the back seat of a car, you never know when you'll explode.

Why is a WASP's sex life different from ours?

When he says, "Let's eat out," they go to a restaurant.

Did you hear about the Polack who died of shit in his veins?

He'd been shooting craps.

Where do they imprison blacks?

In sickle cells.

Why did the black dude hold a lighter under his girl friend's vagina?

He was trying to smoke her crack.

Why did the Polack put his daughter's Cabbage Patch doll in the food processor?

He wanted cole slaw.

What does a Polack do with a pound of cocaine?

Snorts a gram and sells the rest to a narc.

Did you hear about the new Lebanese toilet paper?

If it doesn't like your shit, it blows your ass off.

Why shouldn't you eat at a P.L.O. restaurant?

They don't take orders, they just make demands.

What's the difference between a JAP and a terrorist?

A terrorist makes less demands.

Why did the Yuppie turn to drugs?

His shrink told him to find himself and his girl friend told him to get lost.

Why did the S & M freak travel to Lebanon?

He was into bondage.

What do you call a P.L.O. baby?

A little terror.

How many terrorists does it take to change a light bulb?

None. They all stand around and threaten it.

How do you know your cab driver is a terrorist?

You find yourself tied up in traffic.

Why did the black dude smoke some crack before his job interview?

He wanted to be really up for his drug test.

What's so strange about drinking in Beirut?

You stay sober, but the bar gets bombed.

What's the difference between Karate and Judo?

Karate is a martial art. Jew dough is what you use to make bagels.

How do blacks cure insomnia?

They get a job at the Post Office.

Why do black kids torch cars?

They love Hot Wheels.

Why can't you use the bathroom in Afghanistan?

Because the whole country's occupied.

During World War II, Adolf Hitler consulted a clairvoyant to find out what the future held. The clairvoyant looked into a crystal ball and said, "Mein Fuhrer, I see that you are going to die on a Jewish holiday."

The Fuhrer exploded. "Impossible."

The clairvoyant shrugged. "That is what my vision said."

Hitler demanded, "If it's true, what Jewish holiday will it be?"

"Mein Fuhrer," the clairvoyant answered, "any day you die will be a Jewish holiday."

Why did the Polack bring a box of condoms to school?

The teacher said they were going to study the Trojan War.

The Polack was passing cigars out at the plant after the birth of his son when someone asked, "How much did the kid weigh?"

"Four pounds," replied the Polack.

"Gee, that's small," the guy commented.

"What do you expect?" the Polack said indignantly. "We only been married three months."

A Polish girl received her first high school report card and stormed into the principal's office.

"What are you upset about?" the principal asked. "You deserved to fail Math and English."

"It ain't that," the Polish girl said. "It's up at the top. After 'Sex' it says 'F,' and I didn't even take the fucking course."

A Polack worked only two days as a ditch digger when he went up to the boss and said, "Boss, I can't work. I'm pregnant."

"Pregnant?" the boss exclaimed. "You can't be."

"Yeah?" the Polack said. "Then how come I got labor pains."

Two Mexicans, Pedro and Pancho, had been best friends since birth. Finally, though, Pedro's family decided it was time to marry, so they arranged for a suitable bride. Pancho never even met the girl until the wedding.

Afterwards, at the reception, the tequila flowed like water.

Pedro danced and partied for hours, until he realized that neither Pancho or his bride were in the room. He searched the house.

After a length of time, he finally found his best friend and his wife in the bedroom screwing. He stared for a moment, then broke out laughing hysterically.

The noise attracted several members of his shocked family.

His father glanced in the room, then angrily said to Pedro, "What's so funny?"

"That Pancho," Pedro replied. "He's so drunk, he thinks he's me."

A Polack was cruising down the street in a brand new Cadillac when his friends stopped him and asked him how he got it.

"I was hitchhiking," the Polack said, "when this beautiful girl pulled over and offered me a lift. She drove out into the countryside and parked. We got out of the car and she asked me to kiss her."

"Did you?" a friend asked.

"Yeah," the Polack replied. "Then she stripped down to her panties and told me I could have anything she had."

"So what did you do?"

"I knew the panties wouldn't fit me," the Polack answered. "So I took her car."

An Italian woman went to see the doctor one day and said, "Doctor, I can't take anymore. My husband won't leave me alone and I got eleven kids. I gotta kill myself."

"You can't do that," the doctor said.

"Don't talk to me. I madda up my mind. But I can't jump off no building. You gotta tell me how to do it."

The doctor spent half an hour trying to talk her out of suicide, but in the end he gave in. "Okay," the doctor said. "Go home, get your husband's shotgun and go into the bedroom. Then undress, get into bed, and shoot yourself two inches under your left breast."

The woman thanked him, went home, and blew off her left kneecap.

Why do Japanese women hate oral sex?

When Japanese men smell raw fish, they can't help biting.

How can you tell if a girl in Harlem really loves her baby?

If she waits a few hours after birth before leaving him in a garbage can.

What's the most popular bumper sticker in Southern California?

SAVE THE WHALES: HARPOON A MEXICAN.

How can you tell when a Polish housewife needs to douche?

When the canary dies.

How do you make an Italian girl whistle?

Stick two fingers up her cunt and blow.

How can you tell when Polish parents really love their baby?

Every month, they buy him a new diaper.

Why do Polacks save their used toilet paper?

They hang it up as fly paper.

Did you hear about the Puerto Rican who refused to smoke crack?

He was into classic coke.

Why did the Polish biologist tape his dungarees together?

He wanted to try splicing genes.

Why did the Polish girl fuck her robot?

She wanted to be artificially inseminated.

What's an Italian pay toilet?

When you take a shit, you get money for it.

How can you tell you live in a ghetto?

There's a drug store in your lobby.

What's the most popular after dinner drink at a Mexican restaurant?

Kaopectate.

What do they call a vial of crack and a pipe in Harlem?

Day care.

What's sentiment in Harlem?

Not selling your daughter until she's eight.

Why are drug dealers good for morale in Harlem?

They've given the whole community a shot in the arm.

Why is the music blaring from Cadillacs so loud?

It's coming from your car stereo.

Two black chicks were sitting on the stoop when one noticed the other scratching at her crotch. She thought for a moment, then said, "Girl, why you be itching? You got the crabs?"

"I can't get no crabs."

"What you mean?"

"Leroy done told me I's never gonno get no crabs, 'long as he sticks his Black Flag in me twice a night."

What do you do if you get arrested for selling cocaine?

Hire a crack attorney.

Did you hear about the do-it-yourself Polish Sex Change Kit?

A blonde wig, two falsies, and a meat cleaver.

A Polack walked into the bar around midnight, obviously very angry. He'd already downed three shots when a friend came over and asked him what was wrong.

"It's my wife. I came home tonight and found my wife in bed. Something looked suspicious. I went into the bathroom, and sure enough, there was a guy with no clothes on hiding in the shower."

"Boy," the friend says. "No wonder you're angry."

"That ain't the worst," the Polack said. "That son-of-a-bitch in the shower, he lied his way out of it."

What's an Italian ice?

Lemon sherbert with little black hairs on it.

A black woman was filling out forms at the welfare office. For the question, "Number of children," she replied, "13." But under the listing for "Names," she just put down "Leroy."

The welfare worker reviewed her form and said, "You don't understand. We need the names of all 13 children."

The black woman replies, "You gots it. They all named Leroy."

"That's incredible," the welfare worker commented. "How do you manage to call the one you want?"

"I calls them by their last names," the black woman answered.

Did you hear that they don't have kissing booths at Polish carnivals?

But they do have a booth where a girl will pick your nose for a buck.

A Polack said to a friend, "Boy, it's tough getting laid these days."

"Why don't you go to a hooker?" the friend asked.

"Too expensive. I asked my other buddy and he said a piece cost $30."

"That doesn't sound like too much to me."

"But," the Polack replied, "I don't want a piece. I need a hole."

Why did the Polack wait until he was 64 years old to screw his wife?

Because he'd heard that most married couples have sex just before retiring.

How does a Mexican tell if it's raining?

Calls one of his kids inside and sees if he's wet.

Why was the Polack surprised when people told him his coffee tasted like mud?

He used fresh ground every day.

Why don't Puerto Rican dogs do any tricks?

To teach tricks, you have to be smarter than the dog.

Why don't Italians have to give their kids an allowance so they'll be good?

Italian kids are all good for nothing.

The house lights dimmed after intermission, but instead of the second act the audience heard a grief-stricken theater manager announce, "Ladies and gentlemen, I'm very sorry to have to announce that our leading man suffered a fatal heart attack in his dressing room between acts. We're going to have to cancel the rest of the performance."

A stunned silence came over the crowd until an elderly Jewish woman stood and yelled, "Give him an enema!"

"Madam," the theater manager said, "I said the heart attack was fatal."

"Give him an enema!" she shouted again.

The theater manager became perturbed. "I repeat, our leading man is dead. An enema can't possibly help."

The Jewish woman shrugged her shoulders and said, "It can't hurt."

Two black dudes were waking by a synagogue on Rosh Hashanah when they heard the long, plaintive wail of the ram's horn.

"What's that?" asked the first dude.

"I don't know," the second black said. Just then a Jewish man who'd been walking behind them tapped him on the shoulder and explained, "You've just heard the Jews blowing their shofar."

"Wow!" exclaimed the first black guy. "You people sure know how to treat your help."

The wealthy matron called her black chauffeur in and said, "Washington, I've decided to purchase a dachshund for the house. I'm giving you $100 from petty cash to make the transaction."

Washington shook his head, "Missus, no way you're going to get a good dachshund for $100. You be just wastin' your money."

"How much will it cost?"

Washington replied, "I needs at least $300."

The matron thought a moment, then said, "All right, take $300. But I want the finest dachshund available."

She handed him three one hundred dollar bills. He put the money in his pocket and said, "I'll get you the finest dachshund money can buy. But I's got just one more question."

"Yes?"

"What's a dachshund?"

Cohen and Stein were in the garment business, and they were having their worst year ever. Month after month, ten thousand Madras jackets sat on their racks, and their creditors were closing in like wolves. But just as they were about ready to end it all, the door opened one day and a man announced, "I'm here on a buying trip from Australia. You blokes wouldn't happen to have any Madras jackets, would you?"

Cohen looked at Stein, then said, "Maybe we can dig up a few, if the price is right."

After a couple hours of negotiation, the Australian agreed to buy all ten thousand Madras jackets at a very handsome price.

But just as he was about to leave, he added, "I've got to get home office approval on this purchase. Today's Monday. If you don't get a cable from me by the end of the week, the deal is final."

For the next four days, Cohen and Stein paced back and forth in the office, wincing each time they thought they heard footsteps outside the door. They thought they were home free as the clock struck four on Friday afternoon.

Suddenly, there was a knock at the door and a voice called out, "Western Union." Stein felt so weak he collapsed into a chair. Cohen, his face white, went to the door.

A few long minutes passed. Then Cohen burst into the room, shouting, "Great news! Your sister's dead!"

Did you hear the new Union Carbide company song?

"Ten little, nine little, eight little Indians. . . ."

A Jewish businessman named Feldstein arrived at the Pearly Gates at the same time as a black dude from Harlem. St. Peter greeted the pair, then said, "Welcome to Heaven. We're so happy to have you here that I'm allowed to give you anything you want."

The black guy thought a minute, then said, "I wants a million dollars."

Instantly, a million dollars appeared in the dude's hands.

He walked through the gates smiling.

St. Peter turned to Feldstein and said, "Now, my friend, what is your wish?"

Feldstein said, "I'll need $20 in fake jewelry. And ten minutes alone with that black fellow."

Two Polacks decided to make some extra money in the produce business. They went out into the country in their truck and bought a load of watermelons for a dollar a piece. Then they drove back into the city.

To their delight, they sold out their watermelons in less than an hour, for a dollar a piece. But their glee turned to dismay when they counted their money and discovered they'd made exactly what they spent.

One Polack grunted and turned to the other. "See," he said, "I told you we should have gotten a bigger truck."

Did you hear about the new economy sized Cadillac?

It's for blacks on welfare.

Why did General Motors set up an employment office in Harlem?

It's the best place in the country to find crack salesmen.

What do you call a teenage black kid who turns down a vial of crack?

Dead.

What does a black family do for their daughter on her thirteenth birthday?

Throw her a baby shower.

How can you tell Miss West Virginia at the Miss America Contest?

She's the one with tobacco juice stains running down between her tits.

How dangerous are the cocaine wars in Miami?

Well, this Christmas Bob Hope is flying in to entertain the police.

Why did the squaw finally run away from the reservation?

She read that eating red meat was bad for your health.

What resort do paranoids go to?

Club Dread.

Where in the newspaper do you find Polish obituaries?

Under "Civic Improvements."

What's one idea that never got off the ground?

The Polish Air Force.

What are one million Poles doing in Russia?

Holding up the telephone wires.

What does it mean to "renig?"

To change shifts at a car wash.

Did you hear about the Army's new elite Special Forces Unit made up entirely of Puerto Ricans?

In case of war, they're dropped behind the lines to strip the enemy's tanks.

What's Farm Aid?

One redneck holds down a pig so another redneck can fuck it.

What do you call a black's job resume?

A rap sheet.

Did you hear about the porno movie about a JAP housewife?

It's called "Debbie Does Nothing."

Did you hear about the good news and the bad news for convicts on death row?

The good news is all execution dates have been cancelled; the bad news is that everyone has to smoke four packs a day.

Did you hear about the Polish Space Agency?

It's called NASA.

What's the purpose of vocational education?

To give young blacks and Puerto Ricans a profession to be unemployed from.

Where's the population center of Haiti?

A raft about 50 miles offshore from Miami.

What's the national anthem of Haiti?

"Row, row, row your boat. . . ."

Did you hear about the company that sold 10,000 bathtubs to Haiti?

They're being refitted as passenger ships.

Exactly where are South Africa's "homelands" for blacks?

Anywhere in the country, six feet under.

Why shouldn't you touch a Polack's shoes?

Polacks don't know shit from shinola.

How do you clear out a K-Mart?

Yell, "Immigration!"

Did you hear about the Polack who died cooking dinner?

He put his nose in the microwave.

Why do black men love pussy?

'Cause the inside looks like watermelon and the outside smells like catfish.

What do you call a Polack with diarrhea?

Brain drain.

Why do JAPs make their husbands take them to restaurants?

They love whining and dining.

What does a black girl do for her "sweet sixteen" party?

Takes all five of her kids to Kentucky Fried Chicken for lunch.

Why are black kids so jealous of their Cabbage Patch Dolls?

Cabbage Patch Dolls have birth certificates.

What's a Jewish car accident?

No damage to the automobile, but everyone inside has whiplash.

What's diarrhea in Ethiopia?

Shitting more than once a year.

Why do zoologists study ghetto blacks?

They're the highest form of animal life.

Why did the Polack have to buy two tickets at the zoo?

He was so ugly he needed one to get out.

Did you hear that Bill Cosby wrote a special edition of his book Fatherhood for black men?

It's called Fuck and Run.

What's the definition of a stable black family?

The mother changes men less often than the sheets.

An Italian sailor was out at sea when his wife delivered twins. He arrived back on shore a month later to find that, in his absence, his brother had taken over the chore of naming his babies.

"My brother's an idiot," he complained to his wife. "How could you let him name the kids?"

His wife shrugged.

"All right," the Italian said, "what did he name my daughter?"

"Denise," his wife said.

The Italian thought a moment and said, "That's okay. I like that. Maybe I'm wrong. What did he name my son?"

"Da nephew."

Why did the Polack put a bell around his bull's neck?

Because its horns didn't work.

Did you hear about the Polack who froze to death in Vermont?

He tried to take his pants off over his skis.

What are the rules of the most popular parlor game in Poland?

One Polack leaves the room, and the rest of the Polacks have to guess which one of them it was.

What's the definition of eternity?

A group of Polacks trying to finish a game of Trivial Pursuit.

Why did the Polack stand in front of the mirror with his eyes closed?

He wanted to see what he looked like when he was asleep.

A guy started chatting up an attractive woman sitting alone at the bar. After a few minutes, she got up to go to the Ladies' Room.

He leaned over and motioned to the bartender.

"Listen," he said. "I'm really horny, but this bitch is a tough sell. I'll give you $20 bucks for some Spanish Fly."

"We're out of Spanish Fly," the bartender said. "But for $10, I can sell you some Jewish Fly."

"I've never heard of Jewish Fly. Does it work?"

"Guaranteed," the bartender said.

The guy paid for the Jewish Fly and poured it in the girl's drink. Sure enough, once she had a sip, she got very, very friendly. She stroked his hand, then his arm, then his leg.

Finally, she rubbed her breast against him and said, "What do you say we get out of this place?"

"Great!" the guy exclaimed with a gulp.

"We'll pick up my mother, go shopping, and talk about medical school."

Why do Polish policemen carry surfboards?

In case there's a crime wave.

Did you hear about the guy who asked a Jewish girl out to dinner and had sex that very night?

He jerked off half an hour after he dropped her off.

When do they roll out the red carpet for Polish girls?

When they have their periods.

What's a Polish jacuzzi?

You hop in the Polish bathtub and flush.

What do you call the Jewish Mafia?

The Kosher Nostra.

Chapter Two

GROSS CELEBRITY JOKES

What's the difference between Boy George and a haystack?

You can't always find a needle in a haystack.

Why did Helen Keller marry a black man?

It was easy to read his lips.

Did you hear that Dolly Parton decided to burn her bra?

It took the fire department four days to put out the blaze.

When did Kermit stop dating Miss Piggy?

When she became a ham.

Why didn't Joan Rivers get into trouble for appearing on the Tonight Show topless?

No one wanted to make mountains out of molehills.

What did they wrap Roy Cohn's body in?

A scumbag.

Did you hear Nancy Reagan still hasn't told Ron he's really president?

He thinks he's just playing one on TV.

Why did the London police display 14 syringes and needles?

They were the collected works of Boy George.

Why did President Reagan order the attack on Libya?

To impress Jody Foster.

Why wasn't it a surprise Roy Cohn died of AIDS?

Everyone knew it was dangerous to fuck with him.

Why did Roy Cohn have his choice of sex partners?

A lot of gay men are attracted to the biggest pricks.

Why did all the chic young gays in New York want to sleep with Perry Ellis?

They wanted to get designer AIDS.

Why doesn't Pia Zadora appear in movies any more?

She was over-exposed in her first ones.

Don't you think Bo Derek really dresses like a lady?

Lady Godiva.

Did you hear Kermit the Frog died of trichinosis?

He got it from eating Miss Piggy.

Why is Warren Beatty so difficult to shop for?

What do you get for a man who's had everybody?

Why won't Don Johnson take a hot shower?

It clouds his mirror.

Why did the Boston Celtics think Len Bias was like a wildflower?

Two days after they picked him, he died.

When did the Maryland players suspect Len Bias had a drug problem?

When he tried to snort the free throw line.

Why did Prince Andrew marry Sara Fergusen instead of Koo Stark?

He wanted a woman who was more hip.

Why is the Statue of Liberty surrounded by water?

You would be, too, if you had your hand up for 100 years and nobody let you go.

How do you make the Len Bias All-Star Basketball Team?

You have to be six feet and under.

Where's Len Bias playing basketball now?

I don't know, but it must be stiff competition.

What were Dr. Herman Tarnower's last words?

"Jean, you stupid cunt, you're pointing it the wrong way."

Why didn't the medics know right away that Len Bias was dead?

His brain score was normal—no activity.

How do you know success was getting to Len Bias?

He was starting to crack.

What's the difference between Madonna and Teddy Ruxpin?

Teddy Ruxpin has less fur in his armpits.

Did you hear that Ronald McDonald was arrested for child molesting?

He tried to stuff his Big Mac into a small fry.

Why shouldn't you bet against Dolly Parton?

Everything's stacked against you.

What did they discover when they did the biopsy on Ronald Reagan's colon?

Rock Hudson's wristwatch.

What's the difference between Sunny Von Bulow and President Reagan?

Reagan's been brain-dead longer.

Why do people stay away from Griffin O'Neal?

Nobody wants to be in the same boat with him.

Why did Steve Jobs get fired by Apple Computer?

Conflict of interest. They opened his pants and saw he had a Wang in there.

Why is the United States Football League like a 65-year-old whore?

They both got fucked for $3.00.

How did Lucille Ball get her name?

The studio changed it from "Lucille Fuck."

How did Yoko Ono get her name?

When she was born, her father cried, "Oh, no!", because he couldn't tell her face from her ass.

Why did John Lennon and Yoko Ono have such a strange sex life?

He couldn't tell her face from her ass.

Why was Yoko Ono arrested for looking out the window of her limousine?

The cops thought she was mooning.

What's the most practical gift for Imelda Marcos?

A shoe forest.

Why do you find flies buzzing around President Reagan's head?

Because he's got shit for brains.

Why is Nancy Reagan like a dead camel?

They're both very dry humps.

Did you hear the NFL Players' Association agreed to mandatory drug testing?

They volunteered to take any drug the commissioner could find.

Why is the elephant the symbol of the Republican Party?

The elephant has the world's biggest asshole.

What prayer does Reagan say before cabinet meetings?

"Now I lay me down to sleep. . . ."

What can a politican break without touching?

Campaign promises.

What's the Helen Keller Diet?

You can eat anything you want, because you keep missing your mouth.

What's black on the outside and white on the inside?

Len Bias' nose.

Why is Sunny von Bulow a poor writer?

She ends every sentence with a coma.

How could Nancy Reagan make history by dying?

She'd be the first artificial heart donor.

What's the difference between the Reagan administration and a hooker?

There are always a few ways a hooker won't fuck the public.

What American paid the highest price for his freedom?

Johnny Carson.

Why did Helen Keller have her hand in her panties?

She was telling dirty stories.

Why did Helen Keller's date stick her hand in his pants?

She wanted to go sightseeing.

Why doesn't Gumby ever get laid?

He never gets hard.

What did the Olympic rowing team and Pat Nixon have in common?

They both had quite a stroke.

How do we know Lee Harvey Oswald wasn't Polish?

He didn't hit J.F.K. in the ass.

Why did Nancy Reagan's maid need a repairman?

She was busted.

Where does Jane Fonda sit when she pees?

On Golden Pond.

Why doesn't it matter if Reagan's 75 years old?

If he died in office, who'd notice?

Did you hear that the Reagan administration shipped 1 million empty boxes to Ethiopia?

They were labeled "We Don't Care" packages.

Why did Boy George's outrageous dress lead to his drug addiction?

A lot of people who saw him thought he needed a good smack.

Did you hear Miss Piggy left Kermit?

She got a taste of a real porker's sausage.

What's the inscription on Superman's grave?

"Rust in Peace."

Was Roy Cohn really such a contentious bastard?

Yes. He wouldn't even eat anything that agreed with him.

What woman spends the most money on clothes?

Nancy Reagan. She buys everything for a ridiculous figure.

Why did Nancy Reagan like Rock Hudson?

She's a skeleton and he was in the closet.

What's the difference between Roman Polanski and Jerry Lee Lewis?

Roman Polanski doesn't fuck thirteen-year-old girls who are related to him.

What does the bumper sticker on Roman Polanski's car say?

"Have I Hugged Your Kid Today?"

Did you hear the bad news and the good news about Imelda Marcos?

The bad news is she had her legs amputated after an accident. The good news is she won't miss all those shoes in Manila.

What do you call it when a girl has a date with Ted Bundy?

A one night stand.

What's the only area of the U.S. that's been totally unaffected by acid rain?

Reagan's brain.

Did you hear about Reagan's state visit to South America?

He went to lay a wreath on Joseph Mengele's grave.

Did you hear that the Reagan administration has funded 1,000,000 new jobs for blacks?

The job is "organ donor."

How does Reagan feel about the way South Africa handles racial demonstrations?

Jealous.

Why are astronomers studying Boy George?

Because he's a prominent shooting star.

Why do Klaus and Sunny Von Bulow have a "football" marriage?

He's just waiting for her to kick off.

Did you hear that Klaus von Bulow goes to the hospital every day to have oral sex with Sunny?

He promised his mother he'd always eat his vegetable.

Who was the most obnoxious king in history?

Oedipus—he was a real motherfucker.

Why was Oedipus the perfect son?

Everytime his mother wanted him, he'd cum.

Why is Dr. Ruth Westheimer so lucky?

She doesn't have to get down on her knees to give head.

What's saturated fat?

Rodney Dangerfield in a hot tub.

What happened to Rick Nelson's plane party?

It got crashed.

Was Rick Nelson high when his plane crashed?

Not high enough.

What did they find in the wreckage of Nelson's DC-3?

Precious little Rickey.

What's Prince?

Living proof Johnny Mathis screwed Michael Jackson.

What's brown and hides in the attic?

The Diarrhea of Anne Frank.

How do we know Kermit got AIDS from Miss Piggy?

He croaked.

Why was Renee Richards' medical practice in trouble after her sex change operation?

She'd lost her staff.

Why did Renee Richards quit the ladies' tennis tour?

She found it a lot harder playing without balls.

Why did Goldfinger cover women in gold paint?

He had a gilt complex.

What's so special about Michail Gorbachev?

He's the first premier of Russia who's ever weighed more than his wife.

Chapter Three

GROSS ANIMAL JOKES

Of all the world's men, who have the most girl friends?

Scotsmen. About two hundred in every flock.

Why didn't the farm boy want to bring his girl friend to the high school dance?

She was Bossie.

What's the first thing to remember about fucking a female elephant?

Never let her get on top.

Why aren't Volkswagens allowed in Africa?

Because an elephant will screw anything with a trunk in front of it.

How much did the whorehouse charge the elephant?

$35 for the lay and $350 for the condom.

What happens to female elephants who use sheep as tampons?

They come down with Toxic Flock Syndrome.

What's pink, wet, smells like tuna, and weighs 200 pounds?

An elephant's cunt.

What should you do if an elephant's coming?

Get an umbrella.

What do you do when you see an elephant going?

Swim for your life.

What do you get when you cross a JAP and an elephant?

The world's most expensive nose job.

Why were there so few Indians in the Olympics, when India's the second largest country in the world?

There was no elephant-fucking event.

What's harder than getting a pregnant elephant in a Volkswagen?

Getting an elephant pregnant in a Volkswagen.

What's so bad about being captured by a gross elephant?

He makes you pick his nose.

How bad was this summer's draught down South?

Two trees were destroyed fighting over a dog.

During a recess period, two dogs started fucking in the school yard. Embarrassed, the teacher ordered one of the older boys to break them up. He couldn't do it, and neither could three other boys who tried.

Finally, little Nicky, who was in the third grade, stepped up and said, "I can do it."

The older boys laughed, but the teacher told him he could try. Nicky walked over to the two animals and stuck his finger up the ass of the male dog. Immediately, the dog pulled out and ran away.

"How did you learn to do that?" the teacher asked.

Nicky replied, "That there was old Ben. He can dish it out, but he can't take it."

Mary had a little sheep,
And with the sheep she went to sleep,
The sheep turned out to be a ram,
So Mary had a little lamb.

Who determined that eating lox was dangerous to your health?

The Sturgeon General.

What do you call it when you dream about fucking large animals?

An elephantasy.

Who did the Elephant Man go to for skin treatments?

A pachydermatologist.

What do elephants use for tampons?

Sheep.

Why do elephants have trunks?

Because sheep don't have strings.

Why are an elephant's toes yellow?

He's too big to raise his leg to pee.

Who's two feet tall and has an eight-foot dick?

A guy who's been blown by an elephant.

What are the most sexually frustrated animals in the world?

Camels. Most of them only get one hump.

What do you call a story about fucking a giraffe?

Tall tail.

A puppy was sleeping on the railroad tracks when a train suddenly appeared. The groggy little dog tried to scramble out of the way, but the train ran over his tail, cutting off a small piece. The puppy climbed back up the bank to the tracks to find the missing piece. He reached the top just as a train barrelled down from the other direction and cut off his head.

Moral: Don't lose your head over a little piece of tail.

Who circumsizes whales?

Fore-skin divers.

What do you call a rabbit with crabs?

Bugs Bunny.

Why do elephants throw up after every shit?

You'd throw up, too, if you had to wipe your ass with your nose.

How can you tell an elephant has been screwing your wife?

When her cunt's wider than her hips.

Why aren't elephants allowed on beaches?

They won't keep their trunks up.

When do elephants fuck lions?

When they want some real pussy.

What happens when you cross an elephant with a prostitute?

You get a two ton pickup that never forgets.

An old lady took her beloved cat to the vet and complained that the animal wasn't feeling well. The vet took a look at her and announced, "She's not sick, she's pregnant."

"Impossible," cried the old lady. "Agnes has never been out of the house." She stormed out and took the animal to a second vet. But the second vet made the same diagnosis, and the old lady stormed out again.

When the old lady indignantly related her experiences to a third vet, he asked to visit the cat at home before making his final diagnosis. The vet was sitting in the living room, talking to the old woman, when a big tomcat sauntered in.

"That's it," the vet exclaimed. "That male cat is the reason Agnes is pregnant."

"That's outrageous!" the old woman protested. "I told you, she can't be pregnant. That's her brother."

What's the definition of an animal lover?

A guy who adopts a kid for his dog to play with.

What should you do when you pass an elephant?

Unclog the toilet.

Why do elephants have four feet?

Because six inches isn't enough.

A guy walks into the doctor's office, scratching at his balls. He says to the doctor, "My brother lives with us, and I'm gonna toss him out for fucking her behind my back. Because of him, my wife's given me crabs."

The doctor examined him, then said, "I'd forget about your brother and get rid of the dog."

"Why the dog?"

"Because you don't have crabs, you have fleas."

Chapter Four

GROSS HOMOSEXUAL JOKES

Who are the most sociable people in the world?

Gay men. They all have friends up the ass.

Why do dykes only buy a special brand of lesbian shoes?

On regular shoes, the tongues aren't long enough.

Why did the gay boxer lose so many fights?

He was disqualified for low blows.

What's anal sex?

Man in the moon.

Did you hear about the new gay liberation stamp?

When you lick it, it licks back.

What's gay French toast?

Cum on bread.

Why couldn't the gay student sit down?

His seat was taken right before class.

Why do gays shit in a lead container immediately after sex?

Toxic waste disposal.

Why was the gay sergeant kicked out of the Army?

They found him playing with his privates.

Why is a cruising gay like the space probe Voyager?

Because he wants to penetrate the airspace of Uranus.

Why is a football team like a male model?

To succeed, they both have to have good tight ends.

How do they celebrate Chanukah in San Francisco?

For eight days, eight flaming faggots stand side by side.

How's the mood of the gay community in San Francisco?

They still have that same infectious spirit.

How does a gay know he's horny?

He gets a stiff neck.

Can you catch AIDS from clothing?

Not unless you've got Perry Ellis genes.

How can you tell most theatrical agents are gay?

They like to get behind their young talent and push.

How can you tell if an Australian is a faggot?

If he loves doing it in the Outback.

How do you make a fruit cordial?

Pat him on the ass.

Why is AIDS like your phone bill?

You get AIDS from a male carrier.

A king who had three young daughters issued a statement that any prince in the kingdom who passed certain tests of valor could marry his choice of the three.

One of the daughters was blonde, one was brunette, and one was a red-head.

All the princes in the kingdom tried for the young ladies' hands, but each one met a horrible death. Finally, a prince from a neighboring land rode up to the castle and said to the king, "I am ready for any challenges you lay down."

"You must go to the land of the Huns and bring me back the beard of their fierce leader. Next, you must sail across the deadly sea to the land of the Amazons and capture their princess alive. Finally, you must find and slay the king of all the dragons."

The prince nodded and departed. Nothing was heard from him for over a year. One morning, however, he rode up to the castle. With him was the beard of the leader of the Huns, the Amazon princess, and the head of the king of the dragons.

The king said, "Sir, you have passed the tests. You may have your choice of my daughters. Will you choose the blonde, the brunette, or the red-head?"

The prince chose the king, because this is a fairy tale.

Why did the gay car salesman get fired?

He blew every sales opportunity.

Why is a fancy restaurant like Liberace?

They both get their deliveries in the rear.

Why are cruising gays like cannibals?

If they catch you, they'll eat you.

What's a gay's idea of a Big Mac?

A Whopper that cums on his buns.

What's an orthodox fag?

A guy who only eats kosher weinies.

Why was the 30-year-old gay so sad?

All his friends were dead.

What do you call a fag who creams in his underwear?

Fruit of the Loom.

Why can't gays get auto insurance?

They get rear-ended too often.

Why did the gay guy call his boyfriend "Lollypop?"

He's hard for the first few licks, melts in his mouth, and leaves his face sticky afterwards.

What can you do for a gay who's got AIDS?

Send him a recording of "God Save the Queen."

Why is a guy with AIDS so dull?

If you give him an opening, he'll bore you to death.

How do male prostitutes do?

They make piles.

Why is AIDS like a cold?

You're less likely to catch it if you're wearing rubbers.

How can you tell if an Indian is gay?

All his scalps have handles.

What does "AIDS" stand for?

"Ass Is Diseased, Sorry."

What do you call a gay who's not an AIDS carrier?

A eunuch.

What's the only cure for AIDS?

Homo-cide.

Is cruising around town a sure way to get AIDS?

It depends where you get off.

Why do gays make lousy Santas?

Because they'd rather try on your stockings than fill them.

Did you hear about the gay necrophiliac?

He liked to fuck people's ashes.

How did former NFL star Jerry Smith get AIDS?

After he retired, he changed from a tight end to a wide receiver.

Why was the lesbian disqualified at the swimming meet?

She lapped all the other swimmers.

Chapter Five

GROSS JUVENILE, LEPER, CANNIBAL AND VAMPIRE JOKES

Why shouldn't you piss off a leper?

If he gives you the finger, you have to keep it.

Why don't lepers make good boxers?

One punch, and they're apt to lose their heads.

How does the leper TV station sign off every night?

"It's 11:00 p.m. Do you know where your extremities are?"

What's the high point of a leper wedding?

When the bride and groom exchange ring fingers.

A few weeks after his parents' divorce, little Joey passed by his mother's bedroom. The door was ajar, and when he peeked in, he saw his mother lying naked on the bed, rubbing herself all over as she moaned, "I need a man. I need a man."

The scene was repeated several times over the next month. Finally, one night, Joey got up to use the bathroom. As he passed his mother's room, he saw a guy on top of her, pumping away.

Immediately, Joey turned around and ran back to his room. He stripped off his clothes and jumped on the bed. Then he started rubbing himself all over and moaned, "I need a bike. I need a bike. . . ."

A little boy, the oldest of six kids, was sitting in the kitchen with his parents when he asked, "Dad, why can't trains have little trains like people have little people?"

Immediately, the mother retorted, "Because unlike your father, trains pull out on time."

What kind of music do vampires love?

Ragtime.

To a vampire, why are women like a hockey game?

For both, there's far too long a time between periods.

Why do most vampires live in the South?

They love rednecks.

Why did the cannibal rush over to the cafeteria?

He heard children were half price.

Fred was taking his son Joey to the ball game for the first time, and he wanted to make sure the kid had a good time. Before they went to their seats, Fred stopped at the refreshment stand and bought the kid two hot dogs with mustard and sauerkraut, french fries, and a large coke.

In the first inning, Joey turned to his dad and started to say, "Daddy, I want . . ."

Fred interrupted, "I know, you want popcorn." He motioned the vender over and bought a large bag.

The next inning, Joey said, "Daddy, I want . . ."

Fred stopped him again and bought cotton candy.

The third inning, Joey said, "Daddy, I really want . . ."

"It's ice cream," Fred said. He bought a big cup.

The next inning, Joey turned to Fred and vomited

noisily into his lap.

"What in the hell did you do that for?" the father demanded.

Joey replied, "Since the first inning, I've been trying to tell you I want to throw up."

A Scotsman was washed overboard in the midst of a terrible storm. Hours later, he struggled out of the ocean onto a remote African shore, only to be captured by cannibals.

The cannibals put him in a cage and carried him back to their village. He expected to be put into a pot, but instead, he was given food and water. The next evening, however, the cannibals came by, stuck a spear in his arm, drained off some blood, and went away.

The procedure was the same for a week. Finally, the Soctsman saw the cannibals coming again and he howled, "Ye bastard savages. Put me in a pot and eat me if you will. But you're not sticking me for drinks again."

Why did the cannibals capture the Olympic team?

They love fast food.

Why did the cannibal call the dating service?

Take-out food.

Why don't cannibals eat drug addicts?

Junk food isn't good for them.

How can you tell a cannibal's a fussy eater?

He'll eat arms, but he spits out the pits.

What should you do if a girl leper rolls her eyes at you?

Roll them back.

Why couldn't the leper get a security clearance?

Loose lips.

Why was the leper husband so happy?

His wife talked her head off.

What's a bat cave?

A lady vampire's cunt.

What does a vampire call it when his girlfriend gets her period?

Happy hour.

What do cannibals call paraplegics?

Meals on wheels.

Why can't the leper have sex any more?

Someone told him a joke, and he laughed his balls off.

How can you tell a leper is Polish?

He's got a nose on the end of his finger.

Did you hear about the cannibal who broke into the grammar school?

Two days later, he passed the second grade.

Why did the vampire give his girlfriend a blood test?

To see if she was his type.

Mother came running out of the house when she heard screaming. She saw her little Timmy wrestling with the four-year-old girl from next door. She pulled Timmy off and demanded, "What are you doing to Sally?"

"I was trying to get into her pants."

The mother's face turned red. "Why . . . why were you trying to do that?" she stammered.

"I shit in mine," Timmy replied.

The mother came out into the backyard. Her little eight-year-old daughter was standing a couple of inches from the boy next door. As she approached, she was surprised to see Sally was huffing and puffing in the boy's face.

"What are you doing?" she asked.

Sally replied, "We're playing hospital, and I'm a nurse, just like my big sister Jane."

"What are you doing to Timmy?"

"Just what I heard Jane talk about on the phone last night. He's a doctor, and I'm blowing him."

What's the leper's favorite movie?

"Footloose."

Chapter Six

GROSS RELIGIOUS JOKES

What is an artificial inseminary?

A place where nuns go to get pregnant.

What's a black cherry?

A Negro nun.

What's cherry pop?

What happens when you rape a nun.

What're cherry turnovers?

Nuns leaving the convent.

What's cherry pie?

Eating a nun.

What's cherry jam?

Three guys trying to fuck the same nun.

What's cherries jubilee?

Fourteen nuns in a hot tub.

What're cherry pits?

The hair under a nun's arms.

What's a cherry sucker?

A nun giving you a blow job.

What's cherry juice?

A nun giving you a golden shower.

What would you say about a nun who wiped her ass with her clothes?

I'd say she had a filthy habit.

Why is space a vacuum?

Because God sucks.

What's white and gooey and rains down from above?

The Coming of the Lord.

Why does the Reverend Jerry Falwell believe in the Ten Commandments?

Because there's no commandment against blow jobs.

Did you hear about the progressive Catholic school that started sex education?

They take kids to the zoo to watch monkeys fuck.

Why did the young girl leave the convent?

She learned "nun" really meant "none."

A priest and a rabbi decided to buy a car together, since they couldn't afford new cars on their own. They went down to the local dealership and got a good deal on a new Ford LTD. The day they signed the papers, they made a deal among themselves that the vehicle wouldn't be either Catholic or Jewish.

That night, however, the priest climbed out of bed, went out to the garage, and sprinkled holy water under the hood—totally unaware that the rabbi had heard him.

The next night, the rabbi sneaked out to the garage, got out a hacksaw, and took four inches off the tailpipe.

An elderly Jew was rushed to a Catholic hospital for an emergency operation. A nun asked him who would be responsible for the bill. The old man said, "I've only got one relative, a sister. But she's an old maid who converted to Catholicism and became a nun."

Indignantly, the nun retorted, "We nuns are not old

maids—we're married to Jesus Christ."

"In that case," the Jew said, "send the bill to my brother-in-law."

A Jewish man walks into a jewelry store. He says, "I want to buy a present for my wife." He points to a silver crucifix and asks, "How much?"

"Six hundred dollars," replies the salesman.

"How much would it be without the acrobat?"

Sadie Stein had brought her four-year-old grandson to the beach. He was wearing a cute little sailor suit she'd bought him, and she sat back in her beach chair and bragged to all the other ladies about how cute he looked playing in the sand.

Suddenly, a huge wave roared toward shore, and before the lifeguard could react, the water swept up the boy and pulled him out to sea.

Sadie was frantic. "Please, Lord," she implored. "I know I haven't been to temple in years. But You have to save Jacob. I'll never ask for anything again."

The boy's head popped above water for an instant, then the water swallowed him again. Sadie repeated her prayer. The boy appeared again, then went down for the third time. Sadie fell to her knees, wailing and pounding her fists.

This final prayer was answered. Suddenly, the wave returned to shore and deposited the boy on the beach, shaken but alive. Sadie ran to him, hugged him, then looked him over.

Then a frown appeared on her face. She looked up at the heavens and angrily cried, "Hey, You—he had a hat."

What's two boards, three nails, a hammer and a Jew?

Instant Easter.

What does Jerry Falwell eat when he's constipated?

Moral fiber.

Why couldn't Jesus work for the Red Cross?

It's a non-prophet business.

Chapter Seven

GROSS SENIOR CITIZEN JOKES

How can you tell a really horny old maid?

She masturbates with cucumber seeds.

How can you tell an old maid's been using cucumbers a lot?

When the salad comes, so does she.

What's the definition of a fussy old maid?

One who peels her cucumbers before sitting on them.

How do you know you're losing your figure?

When your grandson asks to ski down your tits.

The old couple kept returning to the sex clinic for therapy. They didn't seem to have any emotional problems, and every time the technicians hooked them up to the wires and let them go at it, they performed perfectly. Finally, the director of the clinic called them in and said, "I can't understand why you keep coming back here. Your sex life is more healthy than nine out of ten people your age."

"Simple," said the old man. "We can't have guests in our room at the nursing home, and we can't afford a hotel room. But Medicaid pays you folks every time."

What should you do when you pull a pair of sticky shorts from your drawer?

Tell Grandma to stop blowing her nose in the clean laundry.

Why did the 22-year-old chorus girl leave her rich 78-year-old husband?

Because she finally couldn't stand old age creeping up on her.

Grandma and Grandpa had arrived for Thanksgiving, and the family sat right down to the table. Grandpa evidently had picked up a cold. He sat, sniffling, for a few minutes. Then he let forth with a big sneeze. To the rest of the family's dismay, he covered his mouth, not his nose, so half the table was sprayed.

The family exchanged glances, but said nothing. Grandpa sneezed a second time, and everyone was even more uncomfortable. Finally, after a third explosion, his oldest daughter said, "Pa, please. Cover your nose when you sneeze."

"You don't want me to do that," Grandpa said.

"Yes, we do. Please."

Grandpa nodded. A couple minutes later, he sneezed again, and true to his word, his hand was over his nose. But his teeth flew out and landed in the mashed potatoes.

The play was nearing its climax when the whole row was disrupted by an old man crawling around on his hands and knees. One very upset man called out, "Pop, get back in your seat."

"Can't," the old man said. "I've lost a caramel."

"You're disturbing the whole theater for a lousy candy. I'll buy you another one if you just sit down."

"Need that one," the old man said.

"What's so special about that caramel?"

"My teeth are in it," the old man said.

What do you call getting blown by a eighty-year-old woman?

Gumballing.

The old man found his life very dull as years went on. He saved some money each week until he had $100. Then he went out and bought himself a very fancy, gleaming pair of alligator shoes. He put the shoes on, rushed home, walked in the door, and said to his wife, "Sophie, do you notice anything different about me?"

She just shrugged.

He went into the bedroom, took off his coat, jacket, and hat and came back out into the living room. "Well, Sophie, what do you see now?"

She glanced over and said in a bored voice, "I told you, I don't see anything different."

Frustrated, he went back into the bedroom and took off every stitch of clothing except his shoes. He returned to his wife and demanded, "Now, you've gotta notice."

Sophie said, "All I see is the same old limp dick."

"That limp dick is pointing toward a brand new $100 pair of alligator shoes."

Sophie grimaced. "Better you should have bought a $100 hat."

What's a garden variety romance?

An old maid uses a cucumber and a carrot.

A very wealthy man who'd been raised in a foster home decided one day to look for his real parents. After months of investigation, he discovered that his father had died, but his mother lived in a nursing home. He went to visit her and they had a tear-filled reunion. He was appalled, however, at the dreadful conditions in the shabby nursing home, so he made arrangements to have her moved to the most expensive place in the country.

The man's mother was astounded by the new place. She had a 25 inch color TV and stereo in her beautifully furnished suite. On her first day, she was helped into a silk dressing gown and she sat down to watch TV. She leaned a little to one side, and instantly a nurse was there to straighten her up.

Later, a gourmet dinner was served to her on fine china. When the woman finished, she began to tip to the side. Again, a nurse was there to help her upright.

Moments later, the son arrived. "Mother, dear," he asked, "how do you like it here?"

"It's lovely," she said. "But there's one problem."

"Tell me," the son said.

"They don't let you fart."

An eighty-three-year-old man walks into St. Patrick's Cathedral, waits his turn, then enters the confessional. The priest blesses him, then says, "Tell me your sins, my son."

The old man says, "My wife, she passed away a month ago after 53 years of marriage. Coming back from the funeral, I met this young girl 22 years old. We went home and slept together, and we've been doing it two, three, four times a day since."

The priest asked, "How old are you?"

"83."

"My word," the priest exclaimed. "But at your age, you should know fornication outside marriage is a sin. For your penance you must say ten Hail Mary's and ten

Our Father's."

"I can't," the man said. "I'm Jewish."

"If you're Jewish, why are you here telling me this?"

"I'm telling everybody," the old man replied.

Did you hear about the old man with the horrible case of VD?

All his fingers fell off.

An old man was telling his grandson, "Last winter it got down to 65 below zero, and the heat went off in the house."

"Wow!" the kid exclaimed. "Did your teeth chatter?"

"Don't know," the old man said. "We don't sleep together."

What's an old maid?

A do-it-yourself expert.

Did you hear about the old maid who was tired of candles?

She called in an electrician.

How can you tell you're in an old maid's bathroom?

The plunger's inside the john.

What should you buy your mother on her 65th birthday?

3 carats.

What should you buy your maiden aunt on her 65th birthday?

3 carrots.

What's the only thing that ever gets into an old maid's pants?

A moth.

What's the one advantage of old age?

You can sing and brush your teeth at the same time.

The two old people met at the nursing home and fell in love. The next night, he made his way to her bedroom. She watched him undress in the candlelight, then impatiently watched him fumble around in his pants pocket. "What are you looking for?" she asked.

"My condom," he replied.

"That's ridiculous," she said. "I'm 75 years old. I can't get pregnant."

"I know," he said. "But my doctor told me not to go into damp places without my rubbers."

Did you hear about the new Senior Citizens edition of Trivial Pursuit?

The hardest question is, "Where did you leave your teeth?"

Did you hear about the movie starring a rampaging senior citizen?

It's called, "Gumbo: Tired Blood Part II."

What's the definition of an old maid?

A woman who's been waiting so long for her ship to come in that the pier's collapsed.

Chapter Eight

GROSS SEX JOKES

What do most male executives believe is the most suitable starting position for a female?

Prone.

Do you know that the high divorce rate is largely a function of arithmetic?

Most divorces happen when wives put two and two together.

How do you know your husband is losing interest?

When his favorite sexual position is "next door."

The Italian man went to the doctor for help. His wife had just delivered their tenth bambino, and he didn't want anymore. The doctor gave him a condom, explained how to use it, and sent him home.

Six weeks later, the angry Italian stormed into the doctor's office, swearing and cursing. The doctor finally figured out the man's wife was pregnant again. "Didn't you follow my instructions?" the doctor asked.

"You betch," the Italian said. "You tella me to stretch-a dat over my organ. Only we ain't got no organ, so I stretch-a dat over the piano."

When should you wear a condom?

On every conceivable occasion.

What do a condom and a coffin have in common?

They're both filled with a stiff, only one's coming and the other's going.

The couple had peeled off their clothing and jumped into the sack, when the woman said, "Put a finger in."

He did, and she started to squirm. "Put another finger in," she begged. She writhed even more. "Your hand. Now."

"My hand?"

"Put your hand in."

He did and she started to go wild.

"Put your other hand in," she panted.

"Are you sure?" he asked.

She nodded approval, then groaned with pleasure when he inserted his other hand.

"Now," she cried, "clap."

"I can't."

She looked at him and said, "Tight, huh?"

What would be the best thing about having a woman President in this country?

We wouldn't have to pay her as much.

What's the definition of eternity?

The length of time between when you come and she leaves.

A very snobbish woman was looking in the mirror at the women's club and saying, "You know, I think I look just the way I did on my wedding day."

"That can't be," another member replied. "You're not pregnant."

What do exhibitionists pass out?

Flash cards.

Why did they serve roast donkey at the lodge dinner?

So every guy in the lodge could have a piece of ass.

What do you call a female clone?

A clunt.

Why is sex like a haircut?

You don't know if you'll like it until it's too late to change your mind.

After six years of marriage, Fred's wife was increasingly upset that her husband still insisted on making love in total darkness. Finally, determined to rid him of his hangups, she flipped the light on one night. To her utter amazement, he was screwing her with a dildo in his hand.

"You impotent bastard," she swore. "How dare you fool me like that for six years? You better explain yourself."

"I'll be glad to explain the dildo," Fred replied, "if you'd like to explain our three kids."

After four months at sea, the sailor was so horny he ran from the docks to the nearest hotel. He called the front desk for a girl, took off his clothes, then jumped on the bed. The more he thought about a woman, the more excited he became.

Finally, he heard a knock on the door and in walked a gorgeous blonde. His eyes bugged out as she put down her purse, then did a slow strip, finally revealing every inch of her unbelievable body. She let him gaze for a moment, then asked seductively, "Well, sailor, do you want me to come over there, or do you want to come over here?"

The sailor groaned sadly. "You can come over there. I'm afraid I already came over here."

Is fellatio necessary for perfect sex?

No, but it gives you a head start.

A guy was looking at himself in the bathroom mirror after a shower when he noticed some gray pubic hairs.

"My God," he said, bending over. "I know you haven't been getting much lately, but I didn't realize you were so worried about it."

How do you know when you're flat-chested?

When you lie on your back in the rain and puddles form on your chest.

The couple were undressing in the hotel room when the woman said, "You know, all the guys I've been with have had pet names for their cock—Dick, John, Harry, etc. What do you call your cock?"

The guy said, "My cock doesn't need a name."

"Why not?"

"Because," the guy replied, "even without a name, it always comes when it's called."

What do generals do when they get horny?

Go back to their tent for a few WACS.

A businessman walked into a hotel bar and ordered a martini and a can of tuna fish.

"If you're hungry, sir, I can show you the whole menu," the bartender offered.

"No, thanks," the businessman replied. "I'm not hungry, I'm homesick. Every night at home, I have my martini with my wife."

What's the difference between a nymphomaniac and the wind?

Some days the wind doesn't blow.

Why are men like eggs?

They're either fresh, rotten, or hard-boiled.

Why is a cock nicer than a man?

It always stands up when a woman enters the room.

What's a man on the make?

A guy who ends every sentence with a proposition.

Why did God give women a chin?

So men would have a place to rest their nuts while they're getting a blow job.

What's bigamy?

The same as monogamy—one wife too many.

Why are race car drivers lousy lovers?

All they care about is their pole position.

What's the easiest way to meet someone in a bar?

Pick up their change.

What should you do if your girl friend's no good at fellatio?

Keep pounding it into her head.

Why is it ridiculous for women to say that men make love too fast?

How much speed can you build up in 45 seconds?

A girl walked into the office one morning wearing a full length mink coat. Her girlfriends gathered around her, oooing and ahhhing. Finally, her best friend pulled her aside and said, "Jenny, are you crazy? You don't have that kind of money."

Jenny smiled. "You'd be surprised. I bought this for $500."

Her girlfriend looked at her in amazement. "Where?"

"Best Furs. Ask for Bill."

The next day, the girlfriend went to the fur company. After a couple minutes, Bill walked out. He was tall, rugged, and very good looking. The girlfriend smiled and said, "I'm interested in the mink my friend Jenny bought."

"That's a thousand dollars."

"But Jenny bought it for $500."

Bill moved closer and touched her arm. "Well, I had to go deep into the hole on that one."

The girl nudged his body. "How about taking a licking on this coat?" she asked.

What's Masters & Johnson?

A band-aid company for masochists.

What's bilingual education?

Being Frenched by twins.

What happens when you beat a guy who's into S & M?

He spurts whipped cream.

What device do you use for telephone sex?

A head phone.

What do spermatozoa use diaphragms for?

Trampoline practice.

What do you call it when you spread an inflatable woman's legs?

Dolly partin'.

How can you tell if a witch is horny?

See what end of the broomstick she's riding.

What happens when you get a vasectomy at Sears?

Every time you get an erection, your garage door opens.

An administrator at a Veterans Administration hospital was constantly harassing a number of male orderlies who he suspected of being gay. Every time one of the unfortunate employees was within earshot, he loudly complained about "faggots" and "buttfuckers" being allowed on the payroll.

Finally, one day, the administrator came down with a bad case of stomach flu while at work. Moaning and sick, he was shown to a private room. He was so out of it he didn't notice that the doctor who came to examine him was one of the orderlies he'd been harassing. The "doctor" glanced at his chart, then ordered him to turn over on his stomach so his temperature could be taken. The patient felt a rectal thermometer being inserted, then the doctor left the room.

The patient waited and waited, but the doctor didn't return. He was just about to get up when someone stepped through the door and snapped a photograph.

"Are you a pervert?" the administrator roared. "Haven't you seen anyone's temperature being taken before?"

"Yes," said the photographer. "But I've never seen you with a pansy up your ass."

A guy stopped at a bar on the way home and struck up a conversation with a very well-stacked blonde. Everything seemed to be going nicely until he discovered she was a hooker. He offered her $10, but she wouldn't budge from $50. So he finished his drink and headed home.

That night, the guy and his wife returned to the bar for a couple of drinks. They sat at a table and had just ordered when the blonde came over to the table and said to the guy, "I told you. See what kind of pig you get for your lousy ten bucks?"

A woman walked into a lingerie shop and asked the proprietor about bra sizes.

"We gotta five different size cups," he said. "We got A, we got B, we got C, we got D, and we got V."

"V?" the woman quizzed. "What's size V?"

The proprietor held his arms out wide. "Dat's a va-va-va-VOOM!"

What happens to girls who look for trouble?

They usually get a belly full.

How can you tell a hooker from a hitchhiker?

A hooker is willing to go either way.

Why did the woman call her husband "filet?"

Because he had practically no bone.

Why shouldn't you ever marry a mailman?

He never comes at the right time, and half the time he puts it in somebody else's box.

How do you know you have an ugly wife?

When you move into a new apartment and the neighbors chip in for curtains.

Why can't you sell insurance to a eunuch?

Because he's fixed for life.

How does a girl get to be a Dallas Cowboy cheerleader?

She just has to make the team.

Who's the richest man in the world?

The guy who invented the sofa—millions have been made on it.

A group of Marines were temporarily stationed at a military base that adjoined a women's college. The colonel in charge of the Marines paid a visit to the college president.

"I must warn you," the colonel said, "my men have been on maneuvers for months without women. I advise you to lock your students up."

"Nonsense," the college president said. "I've got nothing to worry about." She pointed to her head and said, "My girls have it up here."

"Madam," the colonel replied, "it makes no difference where they have it—my boys will find it."

Who's the horniest male in the world?

A newborn baby—he bawls all day long.

Did you hear about the sleepy bride?

She couldn't stay awake for a second.

Why is a nymphomaniac movie star like a tennis player?

They both like new balls for every set.

Who picks up the used condoms in a whorehouse?

The Rubber Maid.

Where do you find bi-sexual prostitutes?

On two-way streets.

How can you tell a guy loves to eat his wife?

When the lunch he brings to work is a peanut butter and diaphragm jelly sandwich.

What's the difference between The Joy of Cooking and The Joy of Sex?

One's about eating well, and the other's about eating out well.

Did you hear about the old prostitute whose cunt was shot?

She retired, but kept her hand in the business.

What lubricant do they use at orgies?

3-in-1 Oil.

Did you hear about the new offer from the x-rated cable TV service?

You get a vibrator and free installation.

Why is your girlfriend like a bank certificate of deposit?

Both penalize you for early withdrawals.

How can you tell your kid is growing up?

When he stops asking for an all-day sucker and starts looking for an all-night sucker.

What's the difference between being 25 and being 50?

When a pretty girl stares at you, at age 25 you look in the mirror to complement yourself on being goodlooking; at 50, you check to see if your fly is open.

What's another difference between 25 and 50?

When you're up three or four times a night at 25, you're horny; when you're up three or four times a night at 50, it's kidney trouble.

The teacher of a kindergarten class set aside part of each day where the tiny tykes could pretend to be grownups. One day she paired off the boys and girls as husbands and wives, then told them to pretend they were at a cocktail party. The kids sipped apple juice and made small talk for a little while.

Then the teacher saw one little couple heading for the door. "Sally," the teacher said, "you can't just walk out of a party. You have to go up to the hostess, tell her you're leaving, and tell her the reason why."

"Okay," Sally said. She walked up to the teacher and reported, "I'm sorry, but me and my husband have to leave. My husband peed in his pants."

Why did the hooker sign up for a sex education class?

She wanted to find out about better paying positions.

A guy was walking down the street when he was startled to see a beautiful, young nude girl running past him. She was closely followed by two men dressed in white. A moment later, a third man carrying two buckets of sand brought up the rear.

The guy stopped the third man and asked, "What's going on?"

"She just escaped from the mental hospital," the man puffed.

"I see. But why are you carrying the sand?"

"It's my handicap," the man said. "I caught her yesterday."

What happened to the girl who laid the entire football team?

She was named an honorary split end.

A Yuppie entered one of his hangouts to find a beautiful girl he'd dated before sitting in a booth, weeping over a brandy. He sat down opposite her and asked, "Julie, what's wrong?"

"Everything," she sobbed. "My parents were killed in

an automobile accident last week, I was fired from my job, I'm being evicted from my apartment, and I discovered I have terminal cancer."

"That's terrible," he said consolingly. "What about if I take you out Saturday night and cheer you up?"

She shook her head no. "I've decided to kill myself Saturday night."

He shrugged and said, "Well, what about Friday night?"

A beautiful girl walked into the formal dinner on the arm of the scowling old tycoon. She found her place at the table while her escort conversed with the other guests. A woman sitting next to her couldn't help staring at a huge gem hanging on a chain around her neck.

"Excuse me," the woman said, "but I must tell you that is the most beautiful diamond I've ever seen."

"It's the Blanton diamond."

"I'm surprised I've never heard of it before," the woman said. "The history of famous gems is my hobby."

The beautiful girl replied, "Well, the Blanton diamond has a horrible curse connected with it."

"Really?" said the woman with great interest. "What is it?"

The beautiful woman grimaced and gestured toward the old tycoon. "It's Blanton over there."

Did you hear that the company that makes M&Ms just bought the Trojan rubber company?

They're going to make a condom that melts in your mouth.

Why did the real estate broker divorce his wife?

He discovered she was selling lots on the side.

What's the definition of a perfect secretary?

One who never misses a period.

Did you hear about the baseball player who found it easy to get to first base with his female fans?

He was finally thrown out at home.

Why did the nymphomaniac nickname her boyfriend, "Maxwell?"

He was good to the last drop.

Why should you feel sorry for violent husbands?

Their wives get all the breaks.

What's a four letter word for "woman" that ends in "u-n-t?"

Aunt.

The high school kid said to his date, "Let's not go to the movies. Let's stay home and play Carnival."

"What's carnival?"

"You sit on my face and I'll guess your weight."

Why was the high school girl embarrassed?

Her parents found out her boyfriend was a hot dog.

What did the sign on the whorehouse door read?

"We're closed. Beat it."

What's the definition of a perfect date?

A girl who can eat spaghetti with her hands tied behind her back.

What's the difference between a golf course and a woman?

A woman's hole is in the middle of the rough.

What's a religious divorce?

Your wife worships money, and you don't have any.

Why did the newlyweds leave the reception early?

They were really anxious to get their things together.

Why is a wife like a diaper?

She's always on your ass and she's usually full of shit.

What's an anchovy?

A small fish that smells like a finger.

Why is a guy in a singles' bar like the Secretary of State?

They're both involved in piece negotiations.

Why is a cock like a snake?

It's long and thin,
It's covered with skin,
And God only knows what holes it's been in.

Chapter Nine

DISGUSTING

The quarterback on the college football team looked upon himself as a Greek god, and he resented having to undergo the physical exam required at the beginning of the season. When it was his turn to see the campus doctor, he swaggered in and said arrogantly, "Doc, this is a waste of time. If you find anything wrong with me, I'll get you four season tickets on the 50 yard line."

"Fair enough," the doctor replied. He spent nearly half an hour, poking and prodding and listening with his stethoscope. Finally, he even made the quarterback bend over and stuck two fingers up his ass. But he still didn't find anything wrong.

"Give up, doc?" the quarterback smirked.

"One more test. Open your mouth."

When the quarterback complied, the doctor inserted the two fingers he'd used for the rectal exam. The quarterback gagged and vomited noisely on the floor.

"Ah!" the doctor exclaimed. "Weak stomach."

Why is it so dangerous to French kiss with an epileptic girl?

She might swallow your tongue, too.

Did you hear about the new doll for perverts?

It's called the Ravage Patch doll.

What do you get when you cross a Cabbage Patch doll with the Pillsbury dough boy?

A rich bitch with a yeast infection.

The world's best hypnotist was appearing at Madison Square Garden. He had his watch at the end of a long chain, swinging it back and forth and saying, "You're all in my power. You're all in my power."

Twenty thousand people went into a deep trance. The hypnotist called out, "You're chickens."

Immediately, the entire crowd started saying, "Cluck, cluck, cluck," and flapping their arms.

"You're roosters," the hypnotist ordered. The crowd immediately switched into "Cock-a-doodle-dos."

The hypnotist was about to give a third command when he suddenly dropped his watch. It shattered on the stage and he exclaimed "Shit!"

It took a week to dig out the crowd.

What do people into golden showers like for lunch?

Pee soup.

What's more disgusting than a golden shower?

A brown bath.

Did you hear that they have a new form of death by injection in Texas?

A guy with AIDS fucks you in the ass.

What's made of metal, glass, and rubber, and comes in 50,000 parts?

A Lebanese used car.

Did you hear General Motors has announced a new model called the "Beirut?"

It comes with factory installed pipe bombs.

Who are nattiest soldiers in the world?

Lebanese militia—they're always dressed to kill.

Did you hear about the new VD film they're using in elementary schools?

It's called "See Dick Run."

A woman with bruises all over her face stood before the judge, crying, "Your Honor, he gets up every morning and starts knocking me around the bedroom. He hits me in the head with his fist, and sometimes he uses his belt. If I don't fix his meals just the way he likes them, he hits me with a pot or pan. If I talk back to him, he belts me with a beer bottle. You've got to put him in jail, or he'll kill me."

The judge turned to the defendant. "Well, what do you have to say for yourself?"

"You can't believe a word this woman says, Your Honor," the husband replied. "She's obviously punch drunk."

How does a whore know when to stop giving a golden shower?

When she looks down and sees her John is flushed.

Why is AIDS like botulism?

They both come from bad meat in your can.

"Mrs. Jones! Mrs. Jones. Can Johnny come out and play?"

"But you know Johnny has AIDS."

"We know. We just want to watch him ooze."

An Irish woman and an Italian woman lived in the same tenement building. One day the Irish woman bet her friend that she could stick her ass out the window longer.

The Italian woman agreed, so they both sat on the sill with their ponderous posteriors hanging out. Finally, after a couple of hours, the Irish woman's husband came home and asked what was going on. The wife told him about the bet.

"That's fine and dandy. But I need a blowjob," the Irishman said.

"But I'll lose the bet."

"You give me a blowjob and I'll stick my ass out the window. That Italian woman won't know the difference."

So they changed places. A few minutes later, the Italian woman looked over and saw a pair of balls hanging below her friend's ass. "Molly!" she screamed. "You betta get your ass inside. Your guts are starting to spill out!"

How can you tell a baby wasn't wanted?

When it's born with a coat hanger stuck up its ass.

What's the best thing about being the parents of a missing child?

You save a bundle at Christmas.

What's the second best thing about being the parents of a missing child?

Everytime you see the kid's picture on a milk carton, you think about how much money you're saving.

What do you call a fart that comes forth from a dead body?

A stiff wind.

Where do you buy birthday gifts for missing children?

Lost and Found Department.

What do French women do for their men at Christmas?

They use flavored Tampax.

What's one-pocket pool in New Bedford, Massachusetts?

8 Portuguese fishermen rape your girlfriend on the barroom pool table.

How can you tell a tough school?

The school paper has an obituary column.

What's another way you can tell a tough school?

The teachers have graffiti under their skirts.

What's a third way you can tell a tough school?

In biology class, they dissect a janitor.

Why do they have recess in tough schools?

To evacuate the wounded.

What's another way you can tell a tough school?

In shop class, they work on the handicapped.

What's another way to tell a tough school?

The textbooks are in spray paint.

What do they study in sex education in a tough school?

Whoever they drag in off the street.

What's the difference between a pig and a pervert?

A pig farts in her movie seat; a pervert goes over and smells the seat after the show.

What's another difference between a pig and pervert?

A pig won't change her panties until a pervert offers to buy them.

What's another difference between a pig and a pervert?

A pig won't wipe her ass until a pervert offers his hand.

What's the definition of a real loser?

A guy who has a wet dream and gets AIDS.

When should you suspect your kid has a drug problem?

When his pet rock is from Bolivia.

How do pedarasts get little kids to suck their pricks?

By telling them they're cream-filled.

Why can't women work in Polish bakeries?

The government's afraid of yeast infections.

Did you hear the government just located 1,000 missing children?

They were held prisoner in a milk carton factory.

What does a woman get when she marries a bi-sexual?

Marital AIDS.

Why did the sharks eat Christie McAuliffe's genitals first?

They smelled like tuna.

Why were there no showers on the Challenger?

NASA thought the crew could wash up on shore.

What were Christa McAullife's last words?

"I mean Bud Lite."

What's San Francisco Instant Pudding?

An enema.

What does a necrophiliac call closing time at the mortuary?

Happy Hour.

Where do necrophiliacs go on vacation?

Death Valley.

Why did all the Russian necrophiliacs rush to Chernobyl?

They heard about some really hot pieces of ass.

Why are necrophiliacs so unhappy?

The women in their lives are usually rottin'.

What did the necrophiliac get his girl friend for Christmas?

A Gucci body bag.

Who were the first people to have sex in space?

The Challenger astronauts. As soon as they took off, they were fucked.

How did the pervert make cole slaw?

Creamed in a Cabbage Patch Doll.

If you get AIDS from a whore, why can't you sue for malpractice?

Most of them have a six inch deductable.

A drunk was sitting at the bar, staring at his empty glass. He looked puzzled for a moment, then turned to the guy on one side of him and quizzed, "Shay, did you spill beer in my lap?"

"I most certainly did not," the man replied.

The drunk grumbled, then turned to the guy on the other side and accused him of spilling beer in his lap. The second man issued an angry denial.

The drunk looked down at his wet trousers and said, "Just what I sushpected. An inside job!"

The young hillbilly married a girl from the next valley and took her into the mountains for a honeymoon. He'd only been gone one day, however, when he angrily stormed back home to his Pappy.

"Where's your bride?" Pappy asked.

"I done shot her."

"Why?"

"She were a virgin, Paw."

Pappy replied, "You done the right thing, son. If she weren't good enough for her own kin, she ain't good enough for you."

When do necrophiliacs play hard ball?

When the corpse has rigor mortis.

Why aren't there many gay necrophiliacs anymore?

After the AIDS epidemic, most have died of exhaustion.

What do you call it when your 13-year-old daughter leaves home and gets pregnant?

Runaway inflation.

Why did the pizza man rub meatballs on his wife's cunt?

He'd run out of anchovies.

A man was sitting at the breakfast table one morning when his eight-year-old son came up to him and said, "Daddy, I've decided I want to be just like you."

Flattered, his father said, "Son, I'm glad you want to be a lawyer."

"That isn't what I mean," the boy replied. "I mean I want to fuck Mommy."

What's grosser than having your girlfriend pass you her gum when you French kiss?

When she tells you she's not chewing gum.

How can you tell a pervert is a real loser?

When blowing up his inflatable doll gives him a headache.

Mel the lawyer got a call late one night from one of his clients. Half an hour later, he was down at the city jail, where his client Fred was sobbing in a cell.

"Why are you here?" Mel asked.

"It's my wife," sobbed Fred. "She's a lousy mother."

"You were arrested because your wife's a lousy mother?"

"Yeah," Fred replied. "Last night we had one of our big fights. Finally, I threw the baby at her. And that bitch, she's such a lousy mother that she ducked."

Why is your second month in Alcoholics Anonymous always easier than your first?

Because by the second month you're drinking again.

An institution for the mentally retarded arranged for its inmates to attend a baseball game. The director spent days training the retards to obey his commands so there wouldn't be any trouble.

The day of the game was bright and sunny, and the group arrived just before the first pitch. When it was time for the national anthem, the director yelled, "Up, nuts!", and the inmates immediately rose. When the national anthem was over, the director yelled, "Down, nuts!" and the inmates sat.

The game proceeded, and the inmates were well behaved. When the home team made a good play, the director yelled, "Clap, nuts," and the retards applauded just like normal fans.

Things were going so well that the director left his seat to go get a hot dog and a beer. But when he came back, there was a riot going on. The director finally located his assistant and demanded, "What happened?"

"Everything was fine," the assistant said, "until some guy came over and yelled, 'Peanuts!'"

What was the Challenger crew's favorite rock group?

Wham!

What's the only reason you should have sex with a girl with herpes?

Later, you can watch your love grow.

What's the definition of an elegant street walker?

One whose shade of lipstick exactly matches the color of the sores on her mouth.

Why was the whore with VD so worn out?

All she ever did was eat and run.

Why are Thalidomide babies mugged so often?

Everyone knows they're unarmed.

What did the family call its Thalidomide baby?

Flipper.

What has NASA decided to name the new space shuttle?

The Titanic.

Why are Texans so mad at the Russians?

The world's largest outdoor barbeque is now the Ukraine.

What has four wheels and flies?

A dead cripple in a wheelchair.

What's the fastest way to have an abortion?

Masturbate with a python.

How do you get invited to a necrophiliac orgy?

You get an in-grave invitation.

How can you tell your son's being abused at his day care center?

He comes home every night and sits on his pacifier.

How can you tell your daughter's being abused at her day care center?

She won't eat a hot dog unless it's got hair around it.

How can you tell your son's being abused at his day care center?

When you ask him if he'd like a box lunch, he lifts up your skirt.

How can you tell your daughter's being abused at her day care center?

You catch her trying to make a diaphragm out of silly putty.

How did the astronauts react when their booster rocket exploded?

At first they were calm, but a few minutes later they were all broken up.

What goes "suck, suck, suck, suck, splat?"

A Challenger astronaut on the way down.

What do the airlines do with used vomit bags?

Donate them to Ethiopian Relief and take a tax write-off.

What weighs nine pounds, stinks, and glows in the dark?

A dead Russian baby.

What can you do with dead Russian babies?

Tie them to trees and use them as street lights.

What's another use for dead Russian babies?

Stick them on the bumper of your car for headlights.

What's another use for dead Russian babies?

Plant them at the end of the runway for landing lights.

What's another use for dead Russian babies?

Cut off a leg for a flashlight.

Why can't you cut the ear off a dead Russian baby and use it as a nightlight?

Most live Russian babies are blind.

A guy was walking down the street behind a blind man. Suddenly, the blind man's seeing eye dog stopped, lifted his leg, and pissed all over his master's leg. Then, to the amazement of the onlooker, the blind man reached into his pocket and gave the dog a biscuit.

The guy who'd been watching caught up with the blind man at the next corner. He touched him on the arm and said, "Excuse me, but I gotta know. Why did you give your dog a treat after he'd pissed on your leg?"

"I wasn't rewarding him," the blind man growled. "I wanted to find out where his head was so I could kick him in the ass."

Did you hear about the queer deaf mute?

Neither did he.

What did the man say to the one-legged hitchhiker?

"Hop in."

What are two fingers to a girl with bulemia?

Dessert.

How can you tell a Polish girl has bulemia?

After she eats, she sticks two fingers up her ass to shit it all out.